Y0-CHC-307

To our friend Nathan,
Just like Zeke, you
are a part of God's
Wonderful Plan!
Love,
Carol, Dave, Ryan & Kevin

What God Did for
ZEKE
the Little Caterpillar

written by Robert O'Rourke
illustrated by Roberta K. Loman

Library of Congress Catalog Card Number 90-72105
Copyright © 1991, by Robert O'Rourke
Published by The STANDARD PUBLISHING Company, Cincinnati, Ohio
Division of STANDEX INTERNATIONAL Corporation. Printed in U.S.A.

The days are long for Zeke. They are slow, quiet days to think. He is curled up in his snug, chrysalis home. The sunshine warms him.

He remembers another time, another place, another life when he was a caterpillar.

Oh, but he was
busy then . . .

dodging big trucks
on the road,

climbing up tall fence posts,

crawling across
green fields.

ACMEE
TRUCKING

But mostly, Zeke was
busy eating everything . . .

leaves,

grass,

flowers . . .

anything green
and growing!

For Zeke it was
a time for taking !

But all around Zeke
there was giving too!

His favorite tree soaked up sunshine,
but it gave back juicy, red apples.

The big river had little streams
filling it, but it gave water
back to the clouds so
there would be rain.

Even the birds,
who ate hundreds of seeds,
gave back pretty songs.

What could Zeke give?

He thinks as he is curled up in his
chrysalis home. He remembers taking . . .

warm sunshine,
     dewdrops,
          green things.

Zeke knows he can never give back anything like . . .

juicy red apples,
or raindrops,
or happy songs.

But long ago, in the very beginning,
God had a wonderful plan
for all living things.

He planned for trees, rivers, birds, and even little caterpillars like Zeke.

But God's best plan was for you and me.

God gave us all the gift of life. And the purpose of life is to give back to God a very special gift. That gift is a beautiful life!

Everyone can give that gift back to God.

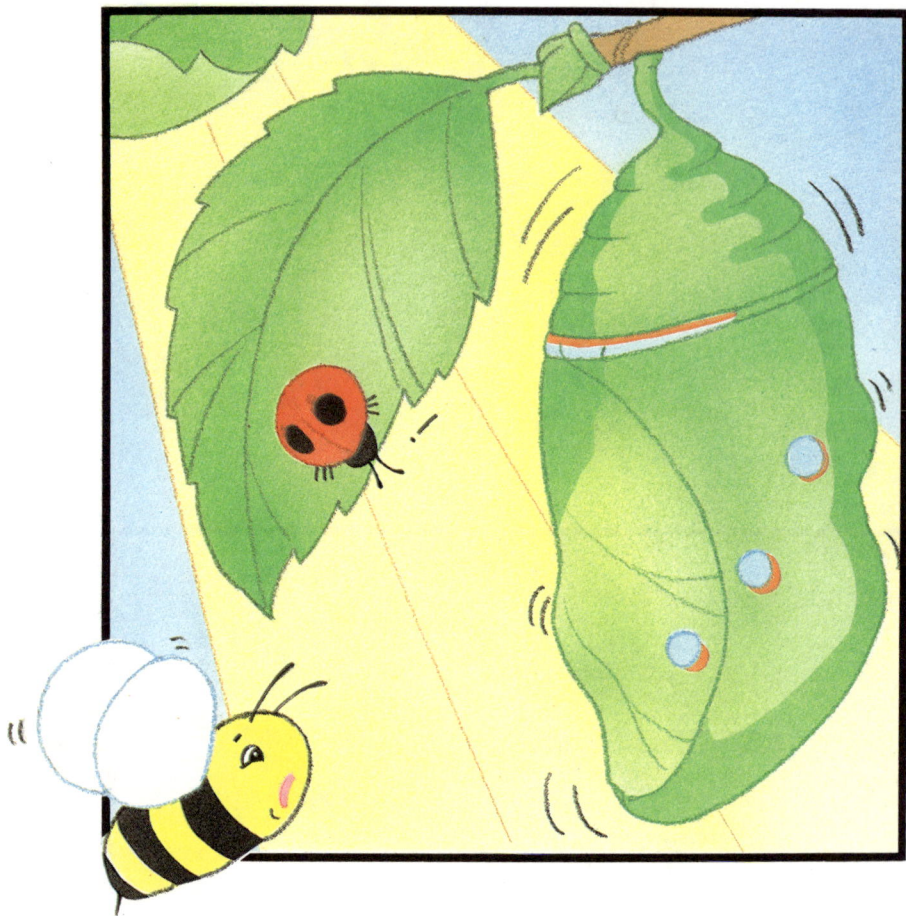

As the sun warms his snug chrysalis, Zeke slowly begins to change. It is as if each ray of sunshine gives him new energy—new life.

He twists and turns.
He strains and pushes.
And suddenly his chrysalis breaks open!

Zeke squeezes out through the hole into a very high limb.

He feels himself all over . . .
Where are his short, stubby legs?
Where has his long, wiggly body gone?

Instead he feels wings and graceful long legs, and big brown eyes.

As Zeke warms in the sun,
he feels zingy and alive.

He wants to . . .

sail on a breeze,

follow a sunbeam,

kiss a flower.

And suddenly it happens . . .
he is part of the world again!

This time Zeke floats over the fields instead of bumping along the ground.

He loves what he is now—
a beautiful butterfly!

Now is his time for giving.

This time, he thinks,
I'll give something special back . . .

not apples,

or rain clouds,

or songs.

This time I will give . . .
bright colors, grace, beauty!

Zeke feels wonderful!